Let's Get C

COOK'S
BIBLE

Over **100** nourishing dishes

igloobooks

igloobooks

Published in 2017
by Igloo Books Ltd
Cottage Farm
Sywell
NN6 0BJ
www.igloobooks.com

Designed by Nicholas Gage
Edited by Jasmin Peppiatt

Food photography and recipe development
© StockFood, The Food Media Agency
Additional imagery © iStock / Getty Images
Cover images: © iStock / Getty Images

REX001 0617
2 4 6 8 10 9 7 5 3 1
ISBN 978-1-78670-489-4

Printed and manufactured in China

Contents

Light Meals

SERVES: 4 | **PREP TIME: 20 MINS** | **COOKING TIME: 1 HOUR 30 MINS**

Minestrone

2 tbsp olive oil
50 g / 1 ½ oz / ⅕ cup pancetta or
    smoked streaky bacon
1 onion, peeled and finely chopped
2 celery stalks, finely chopped
2 carrots, peeled and finely chopped
100 g / 3 ½ oz / ½ cup cauliflower,
    finely chopped
2 cloves garlic, finely chopped
2 potatoes, peeled and finely chopped
1.5 litres / 2 ½ pints / 5 cups
    chicken stock
200 g / 6 ½ oz / ¾ cup greens, such
    as Savoy cabbage, finely sliced
100 g / 3 ½ oz / ½ cup macaroni pasta
salt and pepper
Parmesan cheese
extra virgin olive oil

1. Heat the oil in a large pan and fry the pancetta until the fat runs and it starts to turn golden.

2. Add the vegetables in the order given, giving each one a good 5 minutes to cook without browning, stirring regularly, before adding the next one.

3. Pour in the stock and bring to a gently simmer, then cook very gently for about an hour.

4. Add the greens and the pasta and cook for a further 30 minutes.

5. Adjust the seasoning.

6. Serve hot, warm or even room temperature sprinkled with Parmesan and drizzled with olive oil.

SERVES: 4 | PREP TIME: 10 MINS | COOKING TIME: 25 MINS

Asparagus Risotto

2 tbsp olive oil
40 g butter
1 onion, peeled and finely chopped
1 bunch asparagus, woody ends snapped off
320 g / 11 oz / 1 ⅓ cups risotto rice
100 ml / 3 ½ fl. oz / ½ cup dry white wine
1 litre / 2 ¼ pints / 4 ¼ cups chicken or vegetable stock
salt and pepper
3 tbsp butter
120 g / 4 oz / ½ cup Parmesan, grated
1 lemon, juiced and grated zest

1. Heat the oil and butter in a large pan and add the onion and garlic. Cook until soft and translucent.

2. Chop the asparagus into short lengths and add to the pan. Cook for a few minutes.

3. Add the rice and stir to coat in the butter. Pour in the wine and stir the rice while the wine is absorbed.

4. Once the wine has cooked in, reduce the heat a little and add the hot stock, a ladleful at a time, stirring fairly continuously. This will give the risotto its creamy texture.

5. Keep stirring in the stock and tasting the rice. After about 15–20 minutes, the rice should be soft but with a slight bite. If you've run out of stock before the rice is cooked, simply use water.

6. Season and remove from the heat. Add the butter and Parmesan and leave to melt into the risotto. Stir in the lemon zest and juice.

Gazpacho

800 g / 1 ¾ lb / 3 ⅓ cups ripe tomatoes
10 cm (4 in) piece of cucumber, diced
½ bunch spring onions (scallions), finely chopped
2 cloves garlic, crushed
½ red pepper, finely chopped
1 bunch basil
100 ml / 3 ½ fl. oz / ½ cup extra virgin olive oil
1–2 tbsp red wine vinegar
300 ml ice-cold water
salt and pepper

FOR THE GARNISH
2 spring onions (scallions), finely chopped
10 cm (4 in) piece cucumber, finely chopped
croutons

1. Cut a cross in the skin at the bottom of the tomatoes, place in a bowl of boiling water and leave for 30 seconds. This should help the skins slip off easily.

2. Halve the tomatoes, deseed and chop the flesh and place in a food processor.

3. Add the rest of the ingredients, then whizz until smooth.

4. Pour into a bowl and adjust the seasoning if necessary.

5. Chill thoroughly for at least 1 hour before serving.

6. Check the seasoning and serve with the garnishes.

Satay Chicken

8 chicken thighs, boned and skinned
and cut in half
2 shallots, peeled and finely chopped
½ red chilli, finely chopped
2 cloves garlic, finely chopped
1 cm (½ in) piece fresh ginger, grated
5 tbsp peanut butter
1 tbsp tamarind paste
2 tbsp soy sauce
100 ml / 3 ½ fl. oz / ½ cup coconut milk
1 tsp palm or dark brown sugar
1 tbsp fish sauce
1 lime, juiced

1. Mix together the marinade ingredients and pour half over the chicken pieces.
2. Leave to marinate for at least 4 hours or overnight.
3. Skewer with soaked wooden kebab sticks.
4. Griddle over a high heat until blackened in patches and cooked through.
5. Meanwhile heat the remaining sauce in a small pan, then squeeze in a little lime juice.
6. Serve the satay sauce alongside the chicken.

Leek & Potato Soup

60 g / 2 oz / ¼ cup butter
4 leeks, green ends discarded and
finely sliced
2 floury potatoes, peeled and diced
2 sprigs thyme
850 ml / 1 ½ pints / 3 ½ cups chicken or
vegetable stock
250 ml / 9 fl. oz / 1 cup milk
salt and white pepper
½ bunch chives, chopped

1. In a large pan melt the butter and when foaming add the leeks. Cook gently over a low heat until soft and slithery.
2. Add the potatoes and thyme and cook for a couple of minutes, then add the stock and milk. Bring to a simmer and cook gently for 20–25 minutes, until the potatoes are soft.
3. Remove the thyme stalks and whizz in a blender until smooth.
4. Return to the heat and reheat, seasoning carefully. Serve with chives sprinkled on top.

Herby Fish Cakes

225 g / 8 oz / 1 cup white fish, salmon or
  tuna, cut into small cubes
225 g / 8 oz / 1 cup mashed potato
2 tbsp parsley, chopped
1 tbsp chervil, chopped
3 tsp capers, chopped (optional)
squeeze of lemon juice
salt and pepper
1 egg, beaten
3 tbsp breadcrumbs
vegetable oil

1. Combine the fish, potatoes, herbs, capers and a little lemon juice in a bowl and
   season well.
2. Chill for 30 minutes.
3. Form into equal-sized patties, then dip into the egg, then the breadcrumbs.
4. Heat 1 cm (½ in) depth of oil in a pan and gently fry the fishcakes on both sides
   until golden and crisp.
5. Drain on kitchen paper and serve with peas and ketchup.

Scrambled Eggs on Toast

6 eggs
40 g butter
6 tsp double (heavy) cream
salt and pepper
1 tbsp chives, chopped
4 thick slices bread, toasted and buttered

1. Crack the eggs into a bowl and beat lightly.
2. Heat most of the butter in a pan until foaming, then stir in the eggs.
3. Cook gently, stirring thoroughly with a wooden spoon moving the eggs
   around the pan until lightly cooked with some liquid egg still left.
4. Stir in the cream and chives and season.
5. Serve immediately with the toast.

MAKES: **20** | PREP TIME: **2 HOURS** | COOKING TIME: **15 MINS**

Croissants

625 g / 1 lb 5 oz / 2 ¾ cups strong white (bread) flour
12 g salt
75 g / 3 oz / ⅓ cup sugar
20 g dried yeast
500 g / 1 lb / 2 cups butter, cold, cubed
1 egg, beaten

1. Place the flour, salt, sugar and yeast in a bowl and stir in enough water to make a pliable dough.
2. Tip onto a floured surface, bring together and knead for 5–8 minutes. Refrigerate for 1 hour.
3. After 1 hour, remove the dough from the fridge and roll it out on a floured surface into a 60 x 30 cm (24 x 12 in) rectangle.
4. Roll out the butter into a 20 x 30 cm (8 x 12 in) rectangle and place in the middle of the dough rectangle so it covers two thirds of the dough. Fold the remaining dough third over the butter layer so the dough now has 3 layers. Wrap in cling film and refrigerate for another hour.
5. Flour the work surface and roll the dough out again to 60 x 30 cm (24 x 12 in). Repeat the folding process, then refrigerate again for another hour.
6. Repeat twice more, wrap in more cling film and rest overnight.
7. The next day roll out the dough to around 3 mm thickness and cut into 20 x 20 cm (8 x 8 in) squares.
8. Cut each square in half diagonally to make two triangles and place on a lightly floured surface.
9. Roll each dough triangle up without pressing down too hard and curl round to make the traditional crescent shape. Place on lined baking trays and leave to rise for 1 hour in warm place. Preheat the oven to 200°C (180°C fan) / 400F / gas 6.
10. Lightly brush with beaten egg and bake for about 15 minutes or until crisp.

SERVES: 4 | PREP TIME: 10 MINS | COOKING TIME: 3-5 MINS

Eggs Benedict

4 eggs
4 thick slices ham
4 English muffins
30 g butter

FOR THE HOLLANDAISE SAUCE
175 g / 6 oz / ¾ cup butter
1 tbsp white wine vinegar
2 tbsp lemon juice
3 egg yolks
pinch of salt

1. Melt the butter in a pan. Place the vinegar and lemon juice in another pan and boil.

2. Place the egg yolks and salt in a food processor and whizz briefly, then with it still running, very gradually add the hot lemon juice and vinegar.

3. Again very slowly add the melted butter until the sauce emulsifies.
   Keep warm in a bowl over hot water while you cook the eggs.

4. Poach the eggs in boiling water for about 3 minutes for a runny yolk.
   Remove to kitchen paper and leave to drain.

5. Cut the muffins in half horizontally and lightly toast the cut sides, then butter.

6. Place the muffins on a plate and lay over the slices of ham.

7. Top with the poached eggs and hollandaise sauce.

SERVES: 4 | **PREP TIME: 5 MINS** | **COOKING TIME: 35 MINS**

Cream of Tomato Soup with Basil

500 g / 1 lb / 2 cups ripe tomatoes, halved
olive oil
salt and pepper
rosemary sprigs
4 cloves garlic
1 litre / 2 ¼ pints / 4 ¼ cups
  vegetable stock
100 ml / 3 ½ fl. oz / ½ cup double
  (heavy) cream
1 bunch basil leaves plus stalks

1. Preheat the oven to 200°C (180°C fan) / 400F / gas 7.

2. Tip the tomatoes into a roasting tin and drizzle with oil. Season and tuck the rosemary and garlic cloves in and around.

3. Roast in the oven until blackened and tender – about 25 minutes.

4. Remove the rosemary sprigs and discard. Squeeze the garlic flesh from the skins into a blender and carefully tip in the tomatoes and their juices – you may need to do this in two batches – and the basil stalks.

5. Add the stock and blend until smooth.

6. Return the soup to a pan and heat through with the cream. Heat without boiling, then serve decorate with torn basil leaves.

Stuffed Tomatoes

6 eggs, lightly beaten
40 g butter
6 tsp double (heavy) cream
salt and pepper
1 tbsp parsley, chopped
4 large tomatoes

1. Preheat the oven to 200°C (180°C fan) / 400F / gas 7.
2. Heat most of the butter in a pan until foaming, then stir in the eggs.
3. Cook gently, stirring thoroughly with a wooden spoon moving the eggs around the pan until lightly cooked with some liquid egg still left.
4. Stir in the cream and parsley and season.
5. Core the tomatoes and scoop a little of the flesh from inside, then spoon the egg into the cavity.
6. Place in a roasted tin and cook for 10–15 minutes or until the tomatoes have softened.

Minted Pea Soup

25 g butter
1 onion, peeled and finely chopped
1 garlic clove, finely chopped
250 g / 9 oz / 1 cup peas, fresh or frozen
1 large potato, peeled and chopped
500 ml / 1 pint / 2 cups chicken or
   vegetable stock
¼ bunch mint leaves, chopped
150 ml / 5 fl. oz / ⅔ cup single cream
salt and pepper

1. Heat the butter in a pan and sweat the onion and garlic for about five minutes without browning.
2. Add the peas, potato, stock and half the mint and bring to the boil.
3. Simmer for 5–6 minutes until the peas are tender.
4. Remove and discard the herb stalks and liquidize the soup in a blender until completely smooth.
5. Return to the heat, season and pour in the single cream. Do not allow to boil.
6. Serve in bowls, garnishing with a little chopped mint.

SERVES: 6 | **PREP TIME: 15 MINS** | COOKING TIME: **35 MINS**

Breakfast Frittata

8 eggs
1 tbsp crème fraîche
2 tbsp olive oil
4 good quality pork sausages, meat removed from the skins and cut into small chunks
4 rashers smoked streaky bacon, chopped
100 g / 3 ½ oz / ½ cup button mushrooms, thickly sliced
12 cherry tomatoes, quartered
½ bunch parsley, chopped
salt and pepper

1. Preheat the oven to 180°C (160°C fan) / 350F / gas 5.

2. Beat the eggs with the crème fraîche in a large bowl.

3. Heat the oil in a pan and cook the sausage chunks and bacon until golden.

4. Add the mushrooms and cook briskly until all the liquid evaporates, then add the tomatoes.

5. Pour the egg mixture in and distribute evenly.

6. Bake for about 35 minutes until puffed and golden. The egg should be fully cooked through.

7. Cut into squares and serve warm or cold.

SERVES: 4 | **PREP TIME: 10 MINS**

Prawn Cocktail

1 little gem lettuce, leaves separated
½ cucumber, finely diced
250 g / 9 oz / 1 cup North Atlantic
  prawns (shrimp), cooked

FOR THE MARIE ROSE SAUCE
4 tbsp mayonnaise
2 tbsp tomato ketchup

HOT SAUCE
squeeze of lemon juice
salt and pepper
dash of dry sherry (optional)
½ tsp paprika, to serve

1. Layer the lettuce, cucumber and
   prawns in individual serving glasses.
2. Mix together the ingredients for
   both the sauces, tasting as you go.
   It should not be too sickly.
3. Spoon the sauce over the prawn
   salad, then sprinkle over a little
   paprika before serving.

Noodles with Salmon, Peas & Broccoli

4 nests dried noodles
1 head broccoli, cut into florets
100 g / 3 ½ oz / ½ cup frozen peas
1 tbsp groundnut oil
4 spring onions (scallions), finely chopped
1 cm (½ in) piece ginger, finely sliced
2 salmon fillets, boned and cut into strips
2 tbsp soy sauce
2 tbsp chilli (chili) sauce
1 tsp sesame oil

1. Cook the noodles in boiling salted water according to packet instructions.
2. After 1 minute add the broccoli and peas.
3. Drain well.
4. Meanwhile heat the oil in a wok and add the spring onions and ginger.
5. Sauté for a few minutes, then add the salmon and cook until just pink.
6. Add the noodles and vegetables and pour in the sauces.
7. Toss well to coat, then serve drizzled with sesame oil.

French Toast

1 thick slice white bread per person
2 eggs, beaten
300 ml / 10 fl. oz / 1 ¼ cups full fat milk
   or single cream
1 tsp vanilla extract
½ tsp ground cinnamon
2 tbsp vegetable oil

1. Whisk together the eggs, milk, vanilla and cinnamon and pour into a bowl.
2. Lay the bread into the mixture, soaking it thoroughly for a few minutes.
3. Heat the oil in a pan and gently fry the bread triangles two at a time until golden and crisp on each side.
4. Serve hot.

Smoked Salmon Mousse

250 g / 9 oz / 1 cup smoked
    salmon trimmings
100 g / 3 ½ oz / ½ cup cream cheese
2 tbsp crème fraîche
½ lemon, juiced
2 tbsp chives, chopped
salt and pepper
8–12 slices smoked salmon
lemon wedges to serve

1. Place the ingredients in a food processor and pulse until roughly chopped.
2. Season carefully.
3. Lay 2 slices of smoked salmon out on a surface, overlapping, and place a large spoonful in the centre. Wrap the salmon around the mousse to make an enclosed parcel.
4. Place on a platter, seam side down, and repeat for the remaining salmon slices.
5. Chill until needed then serve with lemon.

Chicken Nuggets

4 chicken breasts, skinned
300 ml / 10 fl. oz / 1 ¼ cups buttermilk
100 g / 3 ½ oz / ½ cup plain
    (all-purpose) flour
2 eggs, beaten
200 g / 7 oz / ¾ cup breadcrumbs
1 tsp mustard powder
pinch of cayenne
1 tsp dried oregano
salt and pepper
vegetable oil

1. Bash the chicken breasts between 2 pieces of cling film with a rolling pin until about 2 cm (1 in) thick.
2. Cut each piece into thick strips and place in a bowl with the buttermilk. Refrigerate for at least 2 hours or even overnight.
3. The next day, dip them one at a time into the flour, egg then breadcrumbs mixed with the flavourings and lay on a rack to dry slightly.
4. Heat 1 cm (½ in) depth oil in a pan and fry the chicken in batches until golden on both sides and cooked through.
5. Serve with a squeeze of lemon and ketchup.

SERVES: 4-6 | PREP TIME: 15 MINS | COOKING TIME: 20-25 MINS

Vegetable Soup

3 tbsp olive oil
1 large onion, chopped
2 carrots, roughly chopped
2 sticks celery, chopped 1 clove garlic, finely chopped
2 large potatoes, peeled and chopped
2 bay leaves
2 x 400 g can chopped tomatoes
1.5 litres / 3 pints / 6 ⅓ cups vegetable stock
large handful green beans, chopped
50 g / 1 ¾ oz / ¼ cup peas
salt and pepper
extra virgin olive oil
parmesan, to serve

1. Heat the oil in a large pan and sweat the onion, carrot and celery until beginning to soften.

2. Add the potatoes, garlic and bay leaves, cook for 3 minutes, then add the tomatoes and stock and bring to a simmer.

3. Cook for 10 minutes then add the beans and peas and leave to simmer for another 6–7 minutes until they are tender.

4. Season well.

5. This soup is best served a little warmer than room temperature with extra virgin olive oil drizzled over and a generous grating of Parmesan.

SERVES: 4-6 | PREP TIME: 10 MINS | COOKING TIME: 40 MINS

Mushroom Soup

50 g / 1 ¾ oz / ¼ cup unsalted butter
1 onion, peeled and finely chopped
500 g / 1 lb / 2 cups flat or wild mushrooms, finely chopped
1 clove garlic, crushed
50 g / 1 ¾ oz / ¼ cup plain (all-purpose) flour
1 glass dry white wine or port
1 litre / 2 ¼ pints / 4 ¼ cups chicken or vegetable stock
salt and pepper
100 ml / 3 ½ fl. oz / ½ cup double (heavy) cream
½ bunch parsley, chopped plus stalks

1. Heat the butter in a large deep pan and sweat the onion without browning for 5–10 minutes or until softened.

2. Add the mushrooms and garlic and cook for a further 5 minutes or until the mushrooms have softened.

3. Stir in the flour and cook out for a few minutes, or until the flour has turned a biscuit colour.

4. Pour over the stock, add the parsley stalks and bring to the boil, stirring constantly.

5. Reduce to a simmer and cook for 10–15 minutes. Remove from the heat and allow to cool a little.

6. Liquidize the soup in batches then return to the pan. Add the seasoning and cream and reheat the soup gently without boiling.

SERVES: 4 | PREP TIME: 30 MINS | COOKING TIME: 30 MINS

Stuffed Peppers

4 ripe red peppers
1 tbsp olive oil
1 onion, peeled and finely chopped
2 cloves garlic, finely chopped
300 g / 10 oz / 1 ¼ cups minced beef
1 tbsp rosemary leaves, finely chopped
2 tbsp tomato purée
200 g / 7 oz / ¾ cup white rice, cooked
2 tbsp Parmesan, grated

1. Cut the tops off the peppers, setting them aside, and hollow out the insides.

2. Fry the onion and garlic in the oil until translucent.

3. Add the beef and rosemary, turn up the heat and fry briskly, stirring, until the beef is cooked. Season.

4. Stir in the tomato purée and a cup of water and leave to simmer until the water is absorbed.

5. Stir in the Parmesan and rice and leave to cool a little.

6. Preheat the oven to 200°C (180°C fan) / 400F / gas 6.

7. Fill the peppers with the beef mixture and place in a roasting tin.

8. Drizzle with olive oil and bake in the oven for about 30 minutes or until they are soft but retaining their shape.

Main Meals

SERVES: 6 | PREP TIME: 45 MINS | COOKING TIME: 20 MINS

Beef Wellington

1 beef fillet, weighing 1 kg / 2 ¼ lb
3 tbsp olive oil
3 tbsp butter
250 g / 9 oz / 1 cup mushrooms
1 shallot, finely chopped
2 sprigs thyme leaves
75 ml / 2 ½ oz / ⅓ cup dry white wine
1 sheet ready rolled puff pastry
1 tbsp flour
2 egg yolks, beaten

TO SERVE
750 g / 1 ⅓ lb / 3 cups new
   potatoes, roasted

1. Preheat oven to 220°C (200°C fan) /
   450F / gas 7.

2. Place the beef in a roasting tin, drizzle
   with oil and roast for 15 minutes.

3. Meanwhile, place the mushrooms in
   a food processor with the shallot and
   process as finely as possible.

4. Heat the butter in a pan and dry the
   mushroom mixture with thyme leaves
   and a little seasoning until softened.
   Add the wine and cook until the wine
   has been absorbed. Set aside to cool.

5. Roll the pastry out a little more on a
   floured surface. Spoon the cooled
   mushrooms over the pastry, leaving
   a small margin around the edges.

6. Place the beef in the centre and roll
   the pastry up like sausage, fully
   encasing the beef. Seal the edges
   with egg yolk, then brush the pastry
   with the remaining egg.

7. Reduce the oven to 200°C (180°C fan)
   / 400F / gas 6 and roast for
   20 minutes until puffed and golden.

8. Delicious served with new potatoes.

SERVES: 4-6 | PREP TIME: 25 MINS | COOKING TIME: 35 MINS

Cottage Pie

2 tbsp vegetable oil
450 g / 1 lb / 2 cups minced beef
1 onion, peeled and finely chopped
2 carrots, peeled and finely chopped
2 sticks celery, finely chopped
100 g / 3 ½ oz / ½ cup flat field
  mushrooms, finely chopped
1 tbsp tomato purée
1 bay leaf
1 sprig rosemary

350 ml / 12 fl. oz / 1 ½ cups beef stock
salt and pepper

FOR THE TOPPING
900 g / 2 lb / 3 ½ cups floury potatoes,
  peeled and cut into chunks
100 g / 3 ½ oz / ½ cup butter

1. Preheat the oven to 180°C (160°C fan) / 350F / gas 4.

2. Heat the oil in a large pan and briskly fry the lamb mince. Add the vegetables and
   sweat until soft.

3. Stir in the tomato purée and cook out for 2 minutes, before adding the herbs and
   pouring over the stock. Simmer until the stock has reduced and there is just a little
   liquid left in the bottom of the pan.

4. Meanwhile cook the potatoes in boiling salted water until tender to the point of
   a knife.

5. Drain thoroughly, then mash until completely smooth with the butter and season well.

6. Pour the lamb base into a baking dish, then spoon over the mashed potato.
   Run a fork down the length of the potato to create edges that will crisp in the oven.

7. Bake for 30 minutes until bubbling and golden.

Beef Meatballs in Tomato Sauce

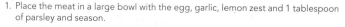

400 g / 14 oz / 1 ½ cups minced beef
1 egg
2 tbsp parsley, chopped
1 clove garlic, crushed
½ lemon, grated zest
salt and pepper
1 thick slice of white bread, crusts removed
  soaked in 2 tbsp milk
3 tbsp olive oil
1 x 400 g can chopped tomatoes
400 ml / 14 fl. oz / 1 ½ cups beef stock
1 tsp sugar

1. Place the meat in a large bowl with the egg, garlic, lemon zest and 1 tablespoon of parsley and season.

2. Mulch the bread in your fingers and crumble into the mix. Mix everything together with your hands to become smooth and sticky.

3. Roll into small walnut-sized balls with cold wet hands, place on a tray and chill for 30 minutes.

4. Heat the oil in a pan and fry the meatballs in batches until brown.

5. Add the tomatoes and stock, then add the sugar and season and bring to the boil. Lower the heat and simmer for about 20 minutes.

6. Serve with pasta or couscous.

Ratatouille

4–6 tbsp olive oil
2 onions, peeled and finely sliced
2 aubergines (eggplants), cut in half
  lengthways and finely sliced
3 courgettes (zucchini), cut in half
  lengthways and finely sliced
2 cloves garlic, finely chopped
3 red peppers, seeded and cut into strips
1 x 400 g can chopped tomatoes
1 tsp coriander seeds, crushed
salt and pepper
handful fresh basil leaves

1. Heat the oil in a pan and cook the onions until deep gold and sweet.

2. Add the aubergines and cook for 2 minutes, then add the courgettes and garlic and cook for 2 minutes, then add the peppers and cook for 5 minutes.

3. Add the tomatoes and coriander seeds and leave to simmer for at least 30 minutes over a very low heat, stirring occasionally, until the vegetables are very soft.

4. Season and sprinkle over the basil before serving.

SERVES: 3-5 | PREP TIME: 5 MINS | COOKING TIME: 1 HOUR 45 MINS

Duck à l'Orange

1 duck, weighing about 2 ¾ kg / 6 lb
salt and pepper

FOR THE SAUCE
100 g / 3 ½ oz / ½ cup caster (superfine) sugar
2 tbsp water
2 oranges, grated zest
250 ml / 9 fl. oz / 1 cup orange juice
1 tbsp marmalade
75 g / 2 ½ oz / ⅓ cup butter, chilled and cubed

1. Preheat the oven to 220°C (200°C fan) / 450F / gas 7.

2. Prick the duck all over with a knife and place in a roasting tin. Season and roast for 20 minutes.

3. Reduce the heat to 180°C / 350F / gas 4 and cook for 1 hour. Remove from the pan, drain to remove excess fat and save the fat for roast potatoes. Rest the duck on a plate.

4. Make the sauce: set the sugar and water in a pan over a low heat and swirl until the sugar has melted. Do not stir. Allow to bubble up until golden.

5. Once dark golden, remove from the heat and carefully, standing back, add any duck resting juices, orange zest and juice.

6. Return to the heat and simmer gently for 10–15 minutes until thickened, stir in the marmalade then whisk in the butter a cube at a time until shiny. Season and serve with the duck.

SERVES: 4 | PREP TIME: 15 MINS | COOKING TIME: 25 MINS

Macaroni Cheese

2 tbsp butter
2 tbsp plain (all-purpose) flour
500 ml / 1 pint / 2 cups milk
1 bay leaf
1 tsp mustard powder
pinch of cayenne
grated nutmeg
150 g / 5 oz / ⅔ cup strong Cheddar
    cheese, grated
salt and pepper
320 g / 11 oz / 1 ¼ cups macaroni pasta

1. Preheat the oven to 180°C (160°C fan)
   / 350F / gas 4.

2. Melt the butter in a pan, then add the
   flour and stir to form a paste.

3. Cook out for a couple of minutes,
   then gradually whisk in the milk to
   form a smooth sauce.

4. Stir in the seasonings and ⅔ of the
   cheese and simmer very gently for
   10–15 minutes to cook out any traces
   of flour.

5. Cook the pasta in boiling salted water
   according to packet instructions.
   Drain thoroughly, retaining a little
   of the cooking water.

6. Tip the pasta into four individual
   ramekins and cover with the cheese
   sauce, adding a little of the cooking
   water to each to loosen.

7. Scatter over the remaining cheese
   and bake for 20–25 minutes until
   bubbling and golden.

Toad in the Hole

300 ml / 10 fl. oz / 1 ¼ cups milk
4 eggs
250 g / 9 oz / 1 cup plain (all-purpose) flour
1 tbsp grain mustard
salt
8 chipolata sausages
4 tbsp vegetable oil or beef dripping

1. Preheat oven to 220°C (200°C fan) / 425F / gas 7.
2. Make the batter: whisk together the eggs and milk and leave to stand for 15 minutes.
3. Heat the oil in a roasting tin and brown the sausages on all sides.
4. Whisk the flour into the milk and eggs then the mustard, then pour into the hot tin around the sausages.
5. Cook in the oven for 20 minutes until golden and billowing. Serve with onion gravy.

Chicken Kiev

4 chicken breasts, skinned
75 g / 2 ¾ oz / ⅓ cup plain
    (all-purpose) flour
3 eggs, beaten
250 g / 9 oz / 1 cup breadcrumbs
4 tbsp vegetable oil
salt and pepper

FOR THE STUFFING
225 g / 8 oz / 1 cup butter, softened
2–3 cloves garlic, crushed
½ bunch parsley, finely chopped
½ bunch tarragon, finely chopped
squeeze of lemon juice

1. Using a sharp knife, cut a pocket in the side of each chicken breast.
2. Mix together the stuffing ingredients until well combined.
3. Use a teaspoon to stuff the pocket with the herb butter, then press the edges firmly together.
4. Place the flour, eggs and breadcrumbs on separate plates. Season the flour.
5. Dip each chicken breast into the flour, eggs then polenta, coating thoroughly each time.
6. Heat the oil then add the chicken breasts and cook, turning regularly for about 20 minutes until cooked through.

SERVES: 4 | PREP TIME: 15 MINS | COOKING TIME: 40 MINS

Spaghetti Bolognese

500 g / 1 lb / 2 cups spaghetti
3 tbsp olive oil
2 onions, peeled and finely chopped
2 cloves garlic, chopped
1 pack pancetta or bacon lardons
500 g / 1 lb / 2 cups minced beef
100 g / 3 ½ oz / ½ cup chicken livers,
  finely chopped
1 glass dry white wine
2 x 400 g can chopped tomatoes
4 tbsp double (heavy) cream
100 g / 3 ½ oz / ½ cup Parmesan, grated
1 bunch parsley, chopped
salt and pepper

1. Heat the oil in a pan and sweat the onion and garlic without browning.

2. Add the pancetta and fry until the fat runs.

3. Add the mince and break it up with a wooden spoon, stirring frequently until browned.

4. Add the chicken livers and cook until browned all over.

5. Season, then add the wine, bubble up, then add the tomatoes.

6. Partially cover and simmer for 20 minutes.

7. Meanwhile cook the pasta in boiling salted water according to packet instructions. Drain and toss with a little oil.

8. Stir the cream and parsley through the sauce, then toss the pasta in the sauce.

SERVES: 4 | PREP TIME: 15 MINS | COOKING TIME: 6 HOURS

Irish Stew

55 ml / 2 fl. oz / ¼ cup sunflower oil
450 g / 1 lb / 3 cups lamb
  shoulder, diced
300 g / 10 ½ oz / 2 cups new potatoes,
  peeled and sliced
2 carrots, peeled and sliced
2 onions, chopped
1 tbsp juniper berries, lightly crushed
2–3 bay leaves

500 ml / 18 fl. oz / 2 cups lamb stock
salt and pepper

TO GARNISH
1 tbsp curly leaf parsley leaves,
  finely chopped

1. Heat half of the oil in a large casserole dish set over a moderate heat until hot.

2. Season the lamb generously and seal in batches until golden brown in colour all over.

3. Transfer the sealed lamb to a slow cooker and reduce the heat under the casserole dish a little.

4. Add the remaining oil and sauté the onions and carrots for 4–5 minutes, stirring occasionally.

5. Add the bay leaves, potatoes, juniper berries, stock and a little seasoning and stir well.

6. Pour on top of the lamb in the slow cooker and stir thoroughly.

7. Cover and cook on a medium setting for 6 hours.

8. Adjust the seasoning to taste after 6 hours and ladle the stew into serving dishes.

9. Garnish with the chopped parsley before serving.

SERVES: **4** | PREP TIME: **35 MINS** | COOKING TIME: **30 MINS**

Peking Duck

4 duck breasts
2 tbsp runny honey
2 tbsp rice vinegar
1 ½ tbsp soy sauce
1 tbsp Chinese 5 spice
1 tbsp soft dark brown sugar

1. Place the duck on a wire rack skin side up and dry thoroughly with kitchen paper. Score the skins with a sharp knife.
2. Mix together the ingredients and brush the skin and leave to marinate for about 30 minutes.
3. Preheat the oven to 190°C (170°C fan) / 375F / gas 5.
4. Brush the duck all over with the sauce and transfer the wire rack to a roasting tin. Pour a cup of water into the bottom of the tin and roast/steam for 30 minutes until the duck is cooked through and the skin is crisp.
5. You can quickly grill the skin if it hasn't crisped up.
6. Serve with rice or pancakes.

SERVES: **4** | PREP TIME: **10 MINS** | COOKING TIME: **20 MINS**

Battered Fish

4 thick fillets white fish such as hake, haddock or cod
a little seasoned flour
225 g / 8 oz / 1 cup self-raising flour
300 ml / 10 fl. oz / 1 ½ cups cold lager
pinch of cayenne pepper
vegetable oil for deep-frying

1. Dust the fish fillets in a little seasoned flour to help the batter stick.
2. Whisk the flour and lager together to make a batter the consistency of double cream.
3. Heat the oil to 180°C / 350F.
4. Dip the fish fillets in the batter, thoroughly coating both sides then cook two at a time for about 10 minutes until deep golden brown and crisp.
5. Keep warm in a low oven while you cook the remaining fish.
6. Serve with lemon wedges, chips and mushy peas.

SERVES: 6 | **PREP TIME: 15 MINS** | **COOKING TIME: 3 HOURS**

Beef Bourguignon

1 kg / 2 ¼ lb / 4 ¼ cups stewing beef, cubed
225 g / 7 ½ oz / 1 ½ cups baby carrots, washed and scrubbed
3 tbsp vegetable oil
1 onion, peeled and sliced
1 tbsp flour
400 ml / 14 fl. oz / 1 ½ cups red wine (preferably Burgundy)
2 cloves garlic, sliced
1 sprig thyme
1 bay leaf
12 pearl or button onions, peeled
225 g / 8 oz / 1 cup smoked streaky bacon, diced
200 g / 7 oz / ¾ cup chestnut mushrooms
salt and pepper

1. Preheat the oven to 140°C (120°C fan) / 275F / gas 1.

2. Sear the beef in 1 tablespoon of oil in a casserole until brown all over. Remove with a slotted spoon.

3. Add the onion and cook until beginning to brown, then return the meat to the pan.

4. Stir in the flour and soak up the juices, then pour in the wine. Add the garlic and herbs, season, cover with a lid and cook for 2 hours.

5. Meanwhile fry the onions and bacon in a little oil, then add, with the mushrooms and carrots to the casserole and cook for 1 more hour.

6. Adjust the seasoning and serve.

SERVES: 3-4 | **PREP TIME: 5 MINS** | **COOKING TIME: 50 MINS**

Lamb Rogan Josh

4 cloves garlic
2 cm (1 in) piece fresh ginger, sliced
4 tbsp vegetable oil
1 tbsp black peppercorns
6 cardamom pods
3 cloves
1 cinnamon stick
1 onion, peeled and finely chopped
750 g / 1 ⅓ lb / 3 cups lamb leg, cubed
    (preferably bone in)
1 tbsp ground coriander
1 tbsp ground cumin
½ tsp cayenne
2 tsp fennel seeds, crushed
2 tsp garam masala
4 tomatoes, chopped
75 ml / 2 ½ oz / ⅓ cup plain yogurt
salt and pepper

1. Whizz the garlic and ginger to a paste in a food processor with a little water.

2. Heat the oil in a large casserole and add the spices. Stir-fry for 2 minutes until fragrant.

3. Add the onion and fry until golden brown, then add the lamb and sear on all sides.

4. Stir in the garlic paste and cook out for a few minutes, then add the ground spices, a little salt and tomatoes, reduce the heat and simmer for 15 minutes or until the sauce is nearly dry.

5. Add enough water to come to nearly the top of the lamb and simmer for about 20 minutes or until the lamb is cooked through.

6. Remove from the heat and stir in the yogurt before serving.

SERVES: **4** | PREP TIME: **20 MINS** | COOKING TIME: **1 HOUR**

Coq au Vin

50 g / 1 ¾ oz / ¼ cup butter
6 rashers smoked streaky bacon or pancetta, diced
2 onions, peeled and finely sliced
3 cloves garlic, finely sliced
2 sprigs thyme
1 chicken, jointed
2 tbsp seasoned flour
300 g / 10 oz / 1 ¼ cups chestnut mushrooms, quartered
600 ml / 1 pint / 2 cups medium white wine, such as Riesling
300 ml / 10 fl. oz / 1 ½ cups double (heavy) cream
salt and pepper
2 tbsp parsley, chopped
squeeze of lemon juice

1. Heat the butter in a casserole and fry the bacon until starting to brown.
2. Add the onion and garlic and cook until lightly gold. Add the thyme.
3. Using a slotted spoon, remove the bacon and onions from the pan to a bowl.
4. Add a little oil. Lightly dust the chicken joints with flour, shake off any excess and brown on all sides in the pan.
5. Add the mushrooms and cook until golden, then return the bacon and onions to the pan.
6. Pour over the wine, bubble up and cook gently for about 30 minutes until the chicken is cooked through.
7. Pour in the cream and parsley, season and add a little lemon juice. Heat until the cream starts to thicken, then serve.

SERVES: **4** | PREP TIME: **20 MINS** | COOKING TIME: **30 MINS**

Paella

5 tbsp olive oil
1 onion, peeled and finely sliced
75 g / 2 ½ oz / ⅓ cup chorizo, diced
2 cloves garlic, finely chopped
1 celery stick, finely chopped
1 red pepper, seeded and sliced
300 g / 10 oz / 1 ¼ cups paella rice
2 chicken thighs, cubed
1 litre / 2 ¼ pints / 4 ¼ cups
  chicken stock

a pinch of saffron threads
1 tsp paprika
4 ripe tomatoes, chopped
50 g / 1 ¾ oz / ¼ cup frozen peas
12 raw prawns (shrimp), shell on
24 mussels, cleaned
2 fillets chunky white fish, skinned,
  boned and cubed
1 lemon, juiced
salt and pepper

1. Heat the olive oil in a large shallow pan and cook the onion, garlic and celery with the chorizo until the orange fat runs.
2. Add the pepper, cook for a further 5 minutes, then stir in the chicken and paella rice and coat thoroughly in the oil.
3. Stir the saffron into the stock then pour it over the rice. Add the paprika. Bring to a simmer and leave uncovered for 10 minutes.
4. Add the tomatoes, peas and seafood and cook for a further 8–10 minutes until everything is just cooked through and the mussels have opened.
5. Stir through the lemon juice, season well and serve.

SERVES: 4 | PREP TIME: 45 MINS | COOKING TIME: 5 MINS

Fresh Gnocchi

700 g floury potatoes, such as
  Maris Piper
250 g plain (all-purpose) flour
1 egg, beaten
salt
nutmeg

1. Boil the potatoes whole and unpeeled
   in boiling salted water for at least
   25 minutes until completely tender.

2. Drain and mash thoroughly or use a
   potato ricer until completely smooth.
   Leave to cool.

3. Tip the cooled potatoes into a bowl
   and work in the flour, egg, a pinch of
   salt and nutmeg until you have a
   smooth dough.

4. Cut the dough in half and roll out to
   make 2 fat sausages.

5. Cut into pieces about 3 cm (1 ¼ in)
   long and press down gently with the
   tines of a fork to make the traditional
   indentations. Place on a floured
   baking sheet to cook when ready.

6. To cook the gnocchi, bring a large
   pan of salted water to the boil then
   add the gnocchi. When they float to
   the top, they are ready, so remove
   and drain on kitchen paper.

SERVES: 4 | PREP TIME: 4 HOURS | COOKING TIME: 3 HOURS

Lamb Tagine

olive oil

2 onions, peeled and sliced

4 cloves garlic, finely sliced

3 preserved lemons

2 x 400 g cans chopped tomatoes

500 ml / 1 pint / 2 cups chicken stock

100 g / 3 ½ oz / ½ cup dried apricots

50 g / 1 ¾ oz / ¼ cup dates

2 tbsp sultanas, 2 tbsp honey

1 bunch coriander (cilantro), chopped

couscous to serve

FOR THE SPICE RUB

½ tsp cayenne

1 tbsp paprika

1 tsp turmeric

2 tsp ground cinnamon

1 tbsp ground cumin

salt and pepper

1 kg / 2 ¼ lb / 4 ¼ cups lamb shoulder,
  cubed

1. Preheat the oven to 160°C (140°C fan) / 300F / gas 2.

2. Mix the spices together in a bowl and toss the cubed lamb in half of the spice mix. Marinade overnight or for at least 4 hours.

3. The next day heat 2 tablespoons of oil in a large casserole or tagine and cook the onions and garlic gently for at least 15 minutes until softened and sweet. Add the spice mix and stir well.

4. Add the lamb to the pan, then the preserved lemons and increase the heat a little to brown.

5. Add the tomatoes, stock and dried fruit with the honey and season. Cover with a lid and bake in the oven for 3 hours until the meat is very tender.

6. When the lamb is tender, adjust the seasoning to taste and stir in the coriander.

7. If desired, serve packed into timbales and remove the moulds before serving.

SERVES: 4 | PREP TIME: 40 MINS | COOKING TIME: 15 MINS

Spinach & Ricotta Cannelloni

12 cannelloni tubes or
12 sheets lasagne

2 tbsp Parmesan, grated
salt and pepper

FOR THE FILLING
2 tbsp butter
olive oil
2 cloves garlic, chopped
¼ nutmeg, grated
1 kg / 2 lb / 4 ½ cups spinach leaves
400 g / 13 ½ oz / 1 ½ cups ricotta

FOR THE TOMATO SAUCE
2 tbsp olive oil
1 clove garlic, chopped
2 x 400 g can chopped tomatoes
½ bunch basil, chopped

1. Preheat the oven to 180°C (160°C fan) / 350F / gas 5.

2. Make the filling: heat the butter in a large pan with a little oil and cook the garlic for 2 minutes. Add the spinach and nutmeg and stir until wilted.

3. Spoon into a sieve and press down firmly with a wooden spoon to extract as much liquid as possible. Once done, finely chop the spinach and leave to cool in a bowl.

4. Stir in the ricotta, Parmesan and seasoning.

5. Spoon into the tubes or onto the lasagne sheets and roll up to make 12 cylinders, then lay in a greased baking dish.

6. Make the tomato sauce: heat the oil in a pan and add the garlic and tomatoes. Leave to simmer, topped up with ½ a can of water, for 10 minutes, then add the basil.

7. Spoon over the cannelloni and bake for around 15 minutes until bubbling.

Tagliatelle Carbonara

500 g / 1 lb / 2 cups tagliatelle

2 tbsp butter

12 slices pancetta or smoked streaky bacon, chopped

4 egg yolks

100 ml / 3 ½ fl. oz / ½ cup double (heavy) cream

2 tbsp Parmesan, grated

1. Cook the pasta in boiling salted water according to packet instructions.
2. Heat the butter in a pan and fry the pancetta until golden.
3. Whisk the egg yolks and Parmesan into the cream.
4. Drain the pasta, return to the pan and, working quickly, scrape the pancetta and butter into the pan and toss.
5. Toss off the heat with the egg and cream mixture then serve immediately.

Caramelized Spare Ribs

2 racks baby back ribs

2 tbsp runny honey

3 tbsp tomato ketchup

1 tbsp black treacle or molasses

2 star anise, lightly crushed

2 tsp English mustard

pinch of chilli (chili) flakes

2 tbsp olive oil

salt and pepper

1. Mix together the marinade ingredients and taste. You may want it sweeter or spicier in which case add more of the chosen ingredients.
2. Coat the ribs thoroughly in the marinade and refrigerate for at least 4 hours or overnight.
3. The next day, preheat the oven to 150°C (130°C fan) / 300F / gas 2.
4. Remove the ribs from the marinade and place in a roasting tin, cover with foil and cook slowly for 2–3 hours until the meat falls from the bone. Baste with any leftover marinade every now and then.
5. To serve, heat a griddle pan until hot and lay the ribs on to caramelize the outside. Season well and serve.

SERVES: 4 | PREP TIME: 20 MINS | COOKING TIME: 2 HOURS 10 MINS

Chilli con Carne

2 tbsp vegetable oil

500 g / 1 lb / 2 full cups stewing
  beef, diced

1 onion, peeled and chopped

2 cloves garlic, finely chopped

1 tsp paprika

1 tsp ground cumin

1 tsp cinnamon

½–1 tsp cayenne pepper or ½ tsp dried
  chilli (chili) flakes

1 x 400 g can kidney beans

1 x 400 g can chopped tomatoes

300 ml / 10 fl. oz / 1 ¼ cups beef stock

20 g dark chocolate, finely chopped

TO SERVE

1 lime, juiced

sour cream

rice

1. Heat the oil in a large casserole
   and cook the beef until browned.
   Remove with a slotted spoon.

2. Add the onion and garlic and fry for
   a further 5 minutes until golden.

3. Add the spices and mix well, then
   pour over the kidney beans, tomatoes
   and stock, add the beef back in and
   bring to the boil.

4. Simmer over a low heat for at least
   2 hours, stirring occasionally, until the
   chilli has thickened and reduced.

5. When the meat is falling apart, stir in
   the chocolate and season.

6. Serve with a squeeze of lime juice,
   sour cream and rice.

SERVES: 4 | PREP TIME: 15 MINS | COOKING TIME: 20 MINS

Beef Stroganoff

2 tbsp butter

1 onion, peeled and sliced

2 cloves garlic, finely sliced

400 g / 14 oz / 1 ½ cups mushrooms, sliced

500 g / 1 lb / 2 cups sirloin or rump steak, thinly sliced

salt and pepper

275 ml / 10 fl. oz / 1 cup sour cream

1 tbsp smoked paprika

TO GARNISH

chopped cornichons

flat leaf parsley

boiled rice

1. Fry the onions and garlic in the butter until golden and sweet then add the mushrooms. Cook until all the liquid has completely evaporated and season to taste. Remove from the pan with a slotted spoon.

2. Increase the heat and fry the beef quickly for 2 minutes, then return the vegetables to the pan and pour in the sour cream and paprika.

3. Bubble up, adjust the seasoning and serve with the garnishes.

SERVES: 4 | PREP TIME: 1 HOUR 30 MINS | COOKING TIME: 30 MINS

Tandoori Chicken

4 skinless chicken breasts, diced
200 ml / 7 fl. oz / ¾ cup basmati rice (use
   a measuring jug), rinsed
400 ml / 14 fl. oz / 1 ½ cups boiling water
½ salad tomato, finely diced
salt and pepper
pinch of ground cinnamon
sprigs of coriander (cilantro)
wooden skewers, soaked in water

FOR THE MARINADE
300 ml / 10 fl. oz / 1 ¼ cups
   natural yogurt
1 tsp ground cumin
1 tsp ground coriander
1 tsp garam masala
1 ½ tsp tandoori chilli powder
1 tsp caster (superfine) sugar
1 clove garlic, minced

1. Prepare the tandoori marinade by mixing together all the ingredients for the
   marinade in a mixing bowl. Add the chicken, mix well, then cover and chill for at
   least 1 hour.

2. Bring the water to the boil in a large saucepan and add the rice. Bring back to the
   boil, then cover and simmer for 10–12 minutes.

3. Remove from the heat and keep the lid in place and set to one side.

4. Preheat the grill to hot. Remove the chicken from the marinade, shaking off any
   excess, and thread onto the wooden skewers.

5. Grill for 8–10 minutes, turning occasionally until lightly charred and cooked through.

6. Place the tandoori chicken skewers on top and garnish with the finely diced tomato,
   sprigs of coriander and a sprinkle of ground cinnamon before serving.

SERVES: 4 | PREP TIME: 15 MINS | COOKING TIME: 20 MINS

Sweet and Sour Pork

500 g / 1 lb pork loin, cubed
1 egg white
2 tsp cornflour
salt
1 tsp sesame oil
1 tbsp vegetable oil
1 carrot, peeled and cut into matchsticks
1 red pepper, deseeded and finely sliced
50 g / 1 ¾ oz / ¼ cup pineapple chunks

FOR THE SAUCE
125 ml / 4 fl. oz / ½ cup pineapple juice
splash of dry sherry or rice wine
2 tbsp tomato ketchup
2 tbsp soy sauce
2 tbsp Chinese vinegar or red
   wine vinegar

1. Slice the pork into strips.
2. Combine the egg white, cornflour, a pinch of salt and sesame oil in a bowl then thoroughly coat the pork strips in the mixture.
3. Heat the vegetable oil in a wok until smoking, then add the coated pork and stir-fry over a high heat until the pork is fully cooked.
4. Remove the pork from the pan and set aside. Discard the oil.
5. Heat the oil in the wok again and stir-fry the vegetables over a high heat for 4 minutes.
6. Mix together the sauce ingredients. Add the pork back to the pan with the sauce, bubble up and serve with white rice.

Stuffed Roast Pheasant

1 pheasant, cleaned and boned out
  (ask your butcher)

FOR THE STUFFING
250 g / 9 oz / 1 cup mild goat's cheese
2 tbsp parsley, finely chopped
1 tbsp thyme leaves
1 clove garlic, crushed
salt and pepper

1. Preheat oven to 200°C (180°C fan) / 400F / gas 6.

2. Lay the pheasant out on a surface and open it out.

3. Mix together the stuffing ingredients, then spread the stuffing out into the cavity of the bird.

4. Season, then roll the bird up into a rough sausage shape and secure with string.

5. Place in a roasting tin and season, drizzle with oil and roast for 30–40 minutes until cooked through and the juices run clear.

6. Leave to rest for 10 minutes before carving.

Homemade Burgers

4 sirloin steaks, minced until coarsely
  ground (ask your butcher)
1 tsp salt
1 tbsp grain mustard (optional)
black pepper
olive oil
4 slices Jarlsberg cheese
1 large tomato, thickly sliced
4 burger buns

1. Season the meat well, mix well with the mustard if using and form into patties around 2 cm (1 in) thick. Refrigerate until needed.

2. Heat a griddle to very hot, then brush the burgers on each side with a little oil. Cook for 3–4 minutes each side, then leave to rest for 5–8 minutes wrapped in foil, the slices of cheese melting on top. Serve in buns topped with tomatoes, red onion and salad.

SERVES: **4** | PREP TIME: **10 MINS** | COOKING TIME: **35 MINS**

Sausages with Onion Gravy

8 sausages
vegetable oil
2 tbsp butter
2 large onions, peeled and thickly sliced
2 sprigs thyme
½ tbsp flour
150 ml / 5 fl. oz / ⅔ cup Marsala or red wine
400 ml / 14 fl. oz / 1 ½ cups beef stock
salt and pepper
1 tbsp grain mustard

1. Preheat the oven to 200°C (180°C fan) / 400F / gas 6.

2. Prick the sausages all over with a fork.

3. Drizzle the sausages with oil in a roasting tin and roast for 30 minutes until browned all over, turning occasionally.

4. Meanwhile heat the butter in a pan and cook the onions with thyme for 15–20 minutes, until deep gold and sweet.

5. Stir in the flour and cook out for 2 minutes, then stir in the wine and stock. Season and simmer for 20 minutes until thickened.

6. Stir in the grain mustard, then serve with the cooked sausages and some mashed potato.

SERVES: 4 | PREP TIME: 25 MINS | COOKING TIME: 2 HOURS 15 MINS

Lamb Hotpot

2 tbsp vegetable oil or dripping
1 kg / 2 ¼ lb / 4 ¼ cups neck of lamb, cut into chops
4 lambs' kidneys, cored and chopped small
4 onions, peeled and chopped
1 tbsp butter
1 tbsp flour
500 ml / 1 pint / 2 cups lamb stock or water
1 tbsp Worcestershire sauce
2 bay leaves
1 kg / 2 ¼ lb / 4 ¼ cups potatoes, peeled and cut into 2 cm slices
salt and pepper
pickled red cabbage, to serve

1. Preheat the oven to 170°C (150°C fan) / 325F / gas 3.

2. Heat the fat in a large casserole and dry the meat in batches until browned.
   Add the kidney and cook alongside. Remove with a slotted spoon and set aside.

3. Adding a little butter, cook the onions until translucent, then stir in the flour to
   make a paste.

4. Whisk in the stock and Worcestershire sauce to make a smooth sauce and bring to
   a simmer. Return the meat and kidneys to the sauce.

5. Add the herbs then top with slices of potato, seasoning the layers, arranging in an
   overlapping pattern.

6. Cover with a lid and bake for 1 ½ hours, then remove the lid and cook for a further
   45 minutes to crisp up the potatoes.

7. Serve with the pickled cabbage.

Sides, Snacks and More

SERVES: 4 | PREP TIME: 10 MINS | COOKING TIME: 15 MINS

Four Cheese Sauce

1 tbsp butter
½ shallot, finely chopped
1 glass dry white wine
400 ml / 13 ½ fl. oz / 1 ½ cups double (heavy) cream
100 g / 3 ½ oz / ½ cup Gruyère, grated
100 g / 3 ½ oz / ½ cup Parmesan, grated
50 g / 1 ¾ oz / ¼ cup blue cheese, such as Roquefort crumbled
50 g / 1 ¾ oz / ¼ cup Cheddar, grated
½ tsp mustard powder
salt and pepper

1. Heat the butter in a pan and sweat the shallot until translucent.

2. Add the white wine and reduce until nearly evaporated.

3. Pour in the cream, heat and stir in the cheeses to melt.

4. Add the mustard powder and season carefully.

SERVES: 4 | PREP TIME: 25 MINS | COOKING TIME: 6-7 MINS

Scotch Eggs

4 eggs + 2 eggs beaten
200 g / 7 oz / ¾ cup sausage meat
200 g / 7 oz / ¾ cup minced pork
1 tbsp parsley, finely chopped
½ tbsp sage, finely chopped
½ tsp ground mace
1 tbsp grain or Dijon mustard (optional)
2 tbsp plain (all-purpose) flour
100 g / 3 ½ oz / ½ cup fine
   breadcrumbs, seasoned with a pinch
   of cayenne pepper
vegetable oil

1. Place 4 eggs in a pan of simmering water. Cook for 1 minute, then cover with a lid, remove from the heat and leave for 5 minutes exactly.

2. When the time is up, remove from the heat and chill.

3. Mix together the meat, herbs, salt and pepper, mustard and mix well. Divide into quarters.

4. Peel the boiled eggs. Place the beaten eggs, flour and breadcrumbs in dishes in a line.

5. Lay a piece of cling film on the work surface and cover with a quarter of the forcemeat. Lay another piece on top and squish until large enough to coat the boiled egg.

6. Roll an egg in the flour then place in the centre of the forcemeat. Encase the egg in the meat. Dip each egg into the flour, then beaten egg then breadcrumbs. Repeat for all 4.

7. Heat the oil and cook the eggs two at a time for 6–7 minutes until crisp and golden.

Tartare Sauce

200 g / 7 oz / ¾ cup mayonnaise
1 shallot
2 gherkins (cornichons)
2 tbsp capers, drained
½ bunch parsley, chopped
½ lemon, juiced
salt and pepper

1. Finely chop the shallot and gherkins.
2. Place all of the ingredients into a bowl, adding the mayonnaise last.
3. Mix well to combine all of the ingredients.
4. Adjust the seasoning to taste using salt and pepper and serve.

Fish Stock

450 g / 1 lb / 2 cups fish trimmings
   and bones
500 ml / 1 pint / 2 cups water
150 ml / 5 fl. oz / ⅔ cup dry white wine
1 onion, cut into quarters
2 sticks celery, chopped
parsley sprigs
1 bay leaf
salt and pepper

1. Place everything in a large pan and bring to a simmer.
2. Simmer gently for 20 minutes.
3. Strain and reserve the stock.

SERVES: **4** | PREP TIME: **15 MINS**

Waldorf Salad

225 g / 8 oz / 1 cup celery sticks, finely chopped
225 g / 8 oz / 1 cup walnuts, toasted under a hot grill
225 g / 8 oz / 1 cup seedless grapes, halved
2 eating apples, cored and thinly sliced
4 tbsp mayonnaise
½ lemon, juiced
salt and pepper
lettuce leaves, to serve

1. Place the celery, walnuts, grapes and apple in a bowl.

2. Mix together the mayonnaise, a little lemon juice and seasoning.

3. Stir into the salad ingredients and serve on the lettuce leaves.

SERVES: 4 | PREP TIME: 15 MINS | COOKING TIME: 12 MINS

Vegetable Couscous

250 g / 9 oz / 1 cup couscous
2 tbsp sultanas
250 ml / 9 fl. oz / 1 cup stock
squeeze of lemon juice
2 tbsp olive oil
1 clove garlic, crushed
2 carrots, peeled and thickly sliced
1 red pepper, finely chopped
1 yellow pepper, finely chopped
handful green beans
150 ml / 5 fl. oz / ⅔ cup vegetable stock
4 tomatoes, chopped
salt and pepper
½ bunch parsley, roughly chopped
2 tbsp pine nuts, toasted

1. Place the couscous in a bowl, cover with the hot stock and cling film the bowl. Leave for 10 minutes or so until tender, then fork through the grains and add the lemon.

2. Meanwhile heat the oil in a pan and sauté the garlic, carrots and diced peppers and toss to coat and cook for 3 minutes.

3. Add the beans and cover with vegetable stock and leave to simmer for 5–8 minutes until all is tender.

4. Add the tomatoes and heat through.

5. Tip the sautéed vegetables into the couscous.

6. Season generously then add the parsley and pine nuts and serve.

SERVES: 4 | **PREP TIME: 30 MINS** | COOKING TIME: **15 MINS**

Pilau Rice

500 g / 1 lb / 2 cups basmati rice
30 g butter
1 onion, peeled and finely chopped
5 cardamom pods, lightly crushed
1 cinnamon stick
6 cloves
saffron soaked in 500 ml / 1 pint / 2 cups vegetable stock
a pinch of salt

1. Wash the rice in a sieve under cold running water, then leave to soak for 30 minutes.
2. Heat the butter in a pan and when foaming add the onion. Cook until golden and sweet.
3. Add the spices and toast lightly, then tip in the rice and stir well to coat in the butter.
4. Pour over the stock and a little salt, bring to the boil and cover with a lid. Turn the heat down and leave to cook for 9–10 minutes.
5. Turn off the heat and leave to stand for 5 minutes. Remove the lid and stir with a fork to separate the grains.
6. Great served with curry.

Breaded Mushrooms

100 g / 3 ½ oz / ½ cup button mushrooms, cleaned
100 g / 3 ½ oz / ½ cup plain (all-purpose) flour, seasoned
1 tsp mustard powder
2 eggs, beaten
100 g / 3 ½ oz / ½ cup fine breadcrumbs
2 tbsp Parmesan, finely grated
vegetable oil for deep frying

1. Lay the flour, eggs and breadcrumbs out in separate dishes, adding the mustard powder to the flour and Parmesan to the breadcrumbs.
2. Dip the mushrooms one by one into each dish, coating thoroughly.
3. Heat the oil to 180°C / 350F and deep fry the mushrooms a few at a time until golden brown all over.
4. Drain on kitchen paper and serve.

Vegetable Stock

2 sticks celery, chopped
1 onion, peeled and chopped
2 carrots, chopped
2 bay leaves
10 black peppercorns
1 bunch parsley stalks, tied
salt

1. Place the vegetables in a pan and cover with 570–850 ml (1–1 ½ pints) cold water.
2. Bring to the boil, reduce the heat and simmer for 30 minutes.
3. Strain. The stock is ready to use.

SERVES: 4 | PREP TIME: 2 MINS | COOKING TIME: 40 MINS

Ultimate Mashed Potato

1 kg / 2 ¼ lb / 4 ¼ cups floury potatoes such as King Edward or Desiree
100 g / 3 ½ oz / ½ cup butter
75–100 ml / 2 ½–3 ½ oz / ⅓ – ½ cup milk, warmed
salt and pepper

1. Cook the potatoes whole in their skins in boiling salted water until tender all the way through – about 30 minutes, but keep checking.
2. Drain thoroughly and leave to cool for 5 minutes, then peel off the skins while still hot.
3. Return the flesh to the pan, mash finely and stir in the butter and enough milk with a wooden spoon to make a light, creamy, smooth mash.
4. Season generously and serve hot.

SERVES: 4 | PREP TIME: 5 MINS | COOKING TIME: 10-15 MINS

Apple Sauce

250 g / 9 oz / 1 cup Bramley apples
250 g / 9 oz / 1 cup Cox apples
1 tbsp sugar (optional, depending on tartness of apples and usage)
2 cloves
2 tbsp water

1. Peel and core the apples and cut into chunks.
2. Place in a pan with the sugar, cloves and water and cover with a lid.
3. Cook over a low heat for 10–15 minutes, checking occasionally, until the apples have 'exploded' to a fine purée and are soft.
4. Beat to a purée, remove the cloves and serve.

Potato Salad

1 kg / 2 ¼ lb / 4 ¼ cups new or salad
  potatoes (such as Anya or Charlotte)
2 sprigs mint
a pinch of salt
200 g / 7 oz / ¾ cup mayonnaise
½ bunch chives, chopped
2 spring onions (scallions), chopped
½ bunch parsley, chopped
salt and pepper

1. Cook the potatoes whole in boiling salted water with the mint sprigs, covered with a lid, for about 20 minutes or until tender.
2. Drain thoroughly.
3. Leave to cool slightly then slice thickly.
4. Mix the mayonnaise with the herbs and seasoning and toss with the potatoes while still warm.

Mint Sauce

1 bunch mint leaves
1 tbsp cider or white wine vinegar
1 clove of garlic, minced
1 tbsp olive oil
½ tsp sugar
½ tsp English mustard
salt and pepper
3–4 tbsp natural yogurt (optional)

1. Chop the mint leaves finely and place in a food processor with the vinegar, garlic, oil, sugar and mustard.
2. Whizz to make a thick sauce.
3. Season to taste.
4. Great served with roast lamb. Add the yogurt if you want a creamier sauce.

SERVES: **4** | PREP TIME: **20 MINS** | COOKING TIME: **10 MINS**

Arancini with Tomato and Mozzarella

60 g / 2 oz / ¼ cup leftover risotto rice, cooked
1 tbsp Parmesan, grated
1 tomato, seeded and finely diced
1 ball mozzarella, cut into small cubes
½ bunch basil leaves
1 tbsp plain (all-purpose) flour
1 egg, beaten
40 g breadcrumbs
vegetable oil, for deep frying

1. Leave the leftover risotto to get completely cold – preferably refrigerated overnight.

2. Stir the tomato and Parmesan through the risotto.

3. Shape into equal balls, pushing a small cube of mozzarella into the centre of each one and shaping the rice around it. If you prefer, you could make finger shapes instead.

4. Lay out the flour, egg and breadcrumbs on separate plates.

5. Dip the risotto balls into the flour, then the egg, then the breadcrumbs. Use one hand and keep the other clean for ease.

6. Heat the oil to 180°C or until a cube of bread sizzles when dunked in.

7. Fry the risotto balls until golden and crisp all over.

8. Drain on kitchen paper.

9. Great served hot or warm with a dip of your choice.

Chicken Stock

1 chicken carcass, (cooked for better flavour) broken up
1 stick celery
1 carrot, chopped
1 onion, peeled and halved and stuck with 2 cloves
6 black peppercorns
1 bouquet garni
1 leek, white part only, chopped

1. Place the bones in a large pan, add the vegetables and cover with water.
2. Bring to the boil, then reduce the heat and leave to cook uncovered for about 3 hours.
3. Skim any fat or scum from the surface from time to time.
4. When done, strain into a large bowl and chill. This will make any fat easy to remove.
5. Store in the refrigerator until needed or freeze for up to three months.

Classic Hollandaise Sauce

2 tbsp white wine vinegar
2 tbsp water
1 slice onion
pinch ground mace
1 bay leaf
6 black peppercorns, left whole
3 egg yolks
180 g / 6 oz / ¾ cup butter at room temperature
squeeze of lemon juice
salt and white pepper

1. Place the vinegar, water, onion, mace, bay leaf and peppercorns in a small pan and reduce to about 1 tbsp. Strain into a bowl, add 1 tablespoon of water.
2. Whisk the egg yolks into the reduction.
3. Place the bowl over a pan of barely simmering water and add a little of the butter, whisking until it has melted.
4. Add the butter a little at a time, whisking continually, until the mixture emulsifies and thickens.
5. Cook very gently for 2 minutes, then add a little lemon juice and season.

Pesto

2 handfuls pine nuts
1 clove garlic, peeled and chopped
2 bunches basil
80 g / 3 oz / ⅓ cup Parmesan, grated
extra virgin olive oil
salt and pepper

1. Add the pine nuts to a frying pan over medium heat and lightly toast for a few seconds until golden.
2. Place in a food processor with the garlic, basil and Parmesan.
3. Whizz the ingredients in a food processor until roughly blended, stirring in enough olive oil to loosen.
4. This pesto will keep in the refrigerator for up to three days.

SERVES: **4** | PREP TIME: **10 MINS** | COOKING TIME: **10-15 MINS**

Sautéed New Potatoes

750 g / 1 ⅓ lb / 3 cups new or salad potatoes such as Charlotte or Anya
5 tbsp olive oil
salt and pepper
½ bunch thyme leaves
2 cloves garlic

1. Parboil the potatoes in salted water for 6 minutes or so, until they begin to soften.
2. Drain thoroughly, set back over a low heat to drive off any excess moisture.
3. Use the end of a rolling pin to lightly crack or crush the potatoes to create crisp edges in the pan.
4. Heat the oil in a pan large enough to hold them in one layer, then add the potatoes.
5. Season well, toss in the thyme and garlic and sauté for around 10–15 minutes until golden and crisp.

SERVES: 4-6 | PREP TIME: 40 MINS

Coleslaw

¼ white cabbage, finely shredded

¼ red cabbage, finely shredded

a pinch of salt

½ red onion, finely sliced

2 carrots, peeled and grated

1 apple, peeled and cut into fine matchsticks

FOR THE DRESSING

6 tbsp mayonnaise

2 tbsp sour cream

2 tbsp grain mustard

1 tbsp lemon juice

pepper

1. Salt the shredded cabbage in a bowl and set aside for 30 minutes.

2. Drain off any excess liquid, then tip into a large bowl.

3. Add the onion, carrots and apple.

4. Mix together the ingredients for the dressing with a pinch of salt and toss the salad thoroughly in it.

5. Serve within 2 hours.

Homemade Chips

4 large baking potatoes, peeled and cut
    into 1 cm (½ in) thick batons
vegetable oil
salt

1. To make the chips, soak well in cold water to remove the starch then
   dry thoroughly.
2. Bring a pan a third full of oil to 140°C / 275F and plunge in the chips, in batches
   if necessary and cook for 10 minutes until pale but starting to look 'cooked'.
3. Remove, drain on kitchen paper.
4. Heat the oil to 180°C / 350F and plunge the chips back in until golden and crisp.
   Remove to kitchen paper, season well and serve hot.

Mushy Peas

4 tbsp olive oil
500 g / 1 lb / 2 cups frozen peas
3 spring onions, (scallions), finely chopped
1 bunch mint leaves, chopped
salt and pepper
1 tsp sugar
30 g butter

1. Heat the olive oil gently in a pan and add the peas and spring onions.
2. Cook until they turn bright vivid green, then add the mint, seasoning and a little sugar.
3. Crush with a potato masher and add the butter.
4. Serve hot.

Oven-baked Wedges

4 large floury potatoes, scrubbed
5 tbsp olive oil
salt
1 tsp paprika
pinch of cayenne pepper
½ tsp celery salt
1 tsp dried oregano
tomato relish or chutney, to serve

1. Preheat the oven to 220°C (200°C fan) / 450F / gas 7.
2. Cut the potatoes into wedges lengthways. Parboil in salted water for 3–4 minutes.
3. Drain thoroughly, then set back over a low heat to drive off any excess moisture.
4. Place on a baking sheet and toss with the oil and seasonings until thoroughly coated.
5. Bake in the oven for about 30 minutes until deep gold and crisp.
6. Drain briefly on kitchen paper.
7. Great served with chutney or relish for dipping.

Cranberry Sauce

500 g / 1 lb / 2 cups fresh cranberries
200 g / 7 oz / ¾ cup sugar
zest and juice of 1 orange
1 tbsp port or cassis

1. Place the ingredients in a pan and add 4 tablespoons of water.
2. Bring to a boil then reduce the heat and cook until the cranberries have burst and the sauce has thickened.
3. Pour into a bowl and check if it needs more sugar – it will thicken further as it cools.

SERVES: **4** | PREP TIME: **40 MINS**

Greek Salad

150 g / 5 oz / ⅔ cup cherry tomatoes
1 cucumber
1 red onion, halved and finely sliced
150 g / 5 oz / ⅔ cup black olives, stoned
200 g / 7 oz / ¾ cup feta cheese
2–3 tbsp red wine vinegar
salt and pepper
1 tsp dried oregano or small handful fresh oregano leaves
6–8 tbsp extra virgin olive oil

1. Halve the cherry tomatoes and place in a bowl with a little salt and a drizzle of olive oil. Leave for up to 30 minutes.

2. Halve the cucumber lengthways, then scrape out the seeds with a teaspoon. Slice the halves into half-moons, then place in a colander, sprinkle with a little salt and leave to drain for 30 minutes.

3. When the tomatoes and cucumber are ready, combine them in a large salad bowl with the olives and crumble in the feta cheese.

4. In a separate bowl, whisk together the vinegar and a little seasoning and the oregano. Then whisk in enough extra virgin olive oil to make a thickened emulsion.

5. Drizzle the dressing over the salad vegetables and toss thoroughly before serving.

Desserts

SERVES: 4 | PREP TIME: 25 MINS | COOKING TIME: 1 HOUR

Crème Caramel

125 g / 4 oz / ½ cup caster (superfine) sugar
2 tbsp hot water
150 ml / 5 fl. oz / ⅔ cup milk
300 ml / 10 fl. oz / 1 cup single cream
4 eggs
40 g soft dark brown sugar
2 drops vanilla extract

1. Preheat the oven to 150°C (130°C fan) / 300F / gas 2.
2. Place the sugar in a stainless steel pan and heat. When the sugar begins to melt, leave to darken to a rich dark gold. Do not stir. Remove from the heat, carefully add the water, and pour into a soufflé dish.
3. Pour the milk and cream into a pan and heat gently.
4. Whisk the eggs, sugar and vanilla in a bowl. When the milk is very hot but not boiling, pour onto the egg mixture, whisking constantly until completely blended.
5. Pour into the soufflé dish and place in a roasting tin. Pour in enough hot water to come two thirds of the way up the sides of the dish.
6. Bake in the oven for 1 hour until set.
7. Remove from the refrigerator 1 hour before serving, then release carefully form the mould onto a plate.

SERVES: **4** | PREP TIME: **1 HOUR** | COOKING TIME: **25 MINS**

Black Forest Gateau

250 g / 9 oz / 1 cup butter, softened
250 g / 9 oz / 1 cup caster (superfine) sugar
150 g / 5 oz / ⅔ cup self-raising flour
3 tbsp cocoa powder
1 tsp baking powder
4 eggs
350 g / 12 oz / 1 ½ cups morello cherry jam (jelly)
1 jar or can bottled cherries and their juice
3 tbsp Kirsch
500 ml / 1 pint / 2 cups double (heavy) cream
50 g / 1 ¾ oz / ¼ cup dark chocolate, grated

1. Preheat the oven to 190°C (170°C fan) / 375F / gas 5. Grease and line two
   20 x 20 cm (8 in) sandwich tins.

2. Mix the butter, sugar, flour, cocoa powder, baking powder and eggs in a food
   processor until smooth.

3. Divide equally between the bake tins and bake for 25 minutes until risen.
   Turn onto a wire rack. Leave to cool completely. Slice the cakes in half horizontally.

4. Heat the jam with the cherries and Kirsch for 5 minutes. Leave to cool. Spread over
   three of the sponges. Whisk 300 ml / 10 fl. oz of the cream to soft peaks.

5. Transfer a cherry-topped sponge to a plate, then smooth on ⅓ of the cream.
   Sprinkle with chocolate.

6. Top with a cherry-topped sponge and repeat, then with the third sponge.
   Place the final clean sponge on top.

7. Whisk the cream to soft peaks. Smooth over the cake top and sides with a palette
   knife. Finish with grated chocolate.

SERVES: **4** | PREP TIME: **2 HOURS** | COOKING TIME: **30 MINS**

Crème Brulée

450 ml / 1 pint / 2 cups double (heavy) cream
100 ml / 3 ½ fl. oz / ½ cup milk
1 vanilla pod, halved
5 egg yolks
2 tbsp caster (superfine) sugar plus enough for the topping
1 strawberry, thinly sliced
1 handful blueberries, washed
1 sprig of mint

1. Preheat the oven to 180°C (160°C fan) / 350F / gas 5.

2. Tip the cream into a pan with the milk. Add the seeds from the vanilla pod and the pod itself. Heat almost to boiling point.

3. Whisk the egg yolks and sugar in a bowl until pale in colour. Pour the hot cream into the egg yolks, whisking constantly. Strain through a sieve and stir well.

4. Sit four ramekins in a roasting tin and divide the mixture evenly between them. Pour in enough hot water to come half way up the sides of the ramekins.

5. Bake for about 30 minutes, until set.

6. Leave to cool on a wire rack, then refrigerate until ready to serve.

7. Sprinkle over a thick layer of sugar and either grill or blowtorch until deep golden and melted. Leave to cool and firm then serve garnished with the sliced strawberry, blueberries and mint.

SERVES: 4 | PREP TIME: 25 MINS | COOKING TIME: 25-35 MINS

Apple and Raisin Crumble

750 g / 1 ⅓ lb / 3 cups apples, peeled, cored and diced

75 g / 2 ½ oz / ⅓ cup raisins, soaked in a little brandy

2 tbsp ground cinnamon

FOR THE CRUMBLE

120 g / 4 oz / ½ cup plain (all-purpose) flour

90 g / 3 oz / ½ cup chilled butter, diced

3 tbsp muscovado sugar

3 tbsp caster (superfine) sugar

1. Preheat the oven to 190°C (170°C fan) / 370F / gas 5.

2. Cook the apples with a little water until soft.

3. Put the flour in a bowl with a pinch of salt.

4. Add the cold cubes of butter and, using the tips of your fingers, work the butter into the flour until the mixture resembles porridge oats.

5. Place the cooked apple and soaked raisins with the cinnamon in the bottom of a baking dish and cover loosely with the crumble mixture.

6. Cook in the oven for 25–35 minutes until golden on top.

MAKES: 12-16 | PREP TIME: 20 MINS | COOKING TIME: 20-30 MINS

Chocolate Chip Cookies

120 g / 4 oz / ½ cup dark chocolate, chopped
150 g / 5 oz / ⅔ cup plain (all-purpose) flour
1 tbsp cocoa powder
1 tsp bicarbonate of (baking) soda
pinch of salt
120 g / 4 oz / ½ cup butter, softened
120 g / 4 oz / ½ cup caster (superfine) sugar
1 egg
350 g / 12 oz / 1 ½ cups chocolate chips, white or dark

1. Preheat the oven to 170°C (150°C fan) / 325F / gas 3.

2. Place the chocolate in a bowl over a pan over simmering water and stir until melted. Set aside to cool.

3. Tip the flour, cocoa powder and bicarbonate into a bowl and stir in the salt.

4. Cream the butter and sugar in a bowl until pale and creamy, then whisk in the melted chocolate.

5. Whisk in the egg, then the dry ingredients, then the chocolate chips.

6. Splodge fairly even amounts onto a lined baking sheet about 6 cm (3 ½ in) apart. Cook for 20 minutes or until an inserted skewer comes out not wet with batter – it won't be clean.

7. Leave to cool then transfer to a wire rack. Best eaten warm and soft.

Cherry Clafoutis

500 g / 1 lb / 2 cups cherries, stoned
125 g / 4 oz / ½ cup plain
   (all-purpose) flour
pinch of salt
50 g / 1 ¾ oz / ¼ cup caster
   (superfine) sugar
3 eggs, beaten
300 ml / 10 fl. oz / 1 ¼ cups milk

1. Preheat the oven to 180°C (160°C fan) / 350F / gas 5.
2. Grease a baking tin with butter or vegetable oil, then place the cherries in the bottom.
3. In a bowl, whisk together the flour, salt and sugar and the beaten eggs until smooth, then whisk in the milk and mix to a smooth batter.
4. Pour the mixture over the cherries and bake for 35–40 minutes.
5. Allow to cool before serving.

Vanilla Custard

300 ml / 10 fl. oz / 1 ¼ cups single cream
3 egg yolks
1 tsp cornflour
1 tbsp caster (superfine) sugar
½ tsp vanilla extract

1. Heat the cream in a pan until nearly boiling.
2. Whisk the egg yolks, cornflour, sugar and vanilla extract.
3. Pour the hot cream into the bowl, whisking all the time, then return to the pan. Whisk over a low heat until the sauce has thickened.
4. If the sauce does start to curdle, simply remove from the heat and whisk vigorously as it cools. It will become smooth again.
5. Delicious served with pies and crumbles.

SERVES: **6** | PREP TIME: **25 MINS** | COOKING TIME: **40–45 MINS**

Lemon Drizzle Cake

120 g / 4 oz / ½ cup butter, softened
175 g / 6 oz / ¾ cup caster
  (superfine) sugar
2 eggs
1 lemon, grated zest
175 g / 6 oz / ¾ cup self-raising flour
100 ml / 3 ½ fl. oz / ½ cup milk

FOR THE SYRUP
2 lemons, juiced
100 g / 3 ½ oz / ½ cup icing
  (confectioner's) sugar

FOR THE GLAZE
½ lemon, juiced
150 g / 5 oz / ⅔ cup icing
  (confectioner's) sugar

1. Preheat the oven to 180°C (160°C fan) / 350F / gas 4. Grease and line a loaf tin.

2. Cream the butter and sugar until pale and creamy, then whisk in the eggs a little at a time.

3. Whisk in the zest, then, using a metal spoon, fold in the flour, salt and then stir in the milk. Spoon into the loaf tin and bake for 40–45 minutes until a skewer comes out clean when poked into the centre. Set aside.

4. Heat the lemon juice and sugar in a pan until the sugar dissolves.

5. Puncture the surface of the cake with a skewer and pour over the hot syrup. Leave to cool completely then remove from the tin.

6. Whisk together the lemon juice and sugar to make the glaze, then drizzle over the top of the cake.

MAKES: 10-12 | PREP TIME: 50 MINS | COOKING TIME: 12 MINS

Gingerbread Men

30 g butter, softened
25 g caster (superfine) sugar
½ tsp bicarbonate of soda
25 g golden syrup
1 egg yolk
125 g / 4 oz / ½ cup plain
   (all-purpose) flour
1 tsp ground ginger
½ tsp mixed spice
mixed sugar balls for decoration
golden syrup

1. Preheat the oven to 180°C (160°C fan)
   / 350F / gas 4.

2. Whisk together the butter and sugar
   until pale, then stir in the bicarbonate,
   syrup and egg yolk.

3. Sieve in the flour and spices, then mix
   with a wooden spoon until the
   mixture comes together in a ball.

4. Roll into a cylinder, wrap in clingfilm
   and chill in the refrigerator for
   30 minutes.

5. Roll out to 1 cm (½ in) thickness and
   cut out gingerbread men with
   appropriate cutters. Place them
   evenly on a lined baking sheet.

6. Bake in the oven for about
   12 minutes, then remove to a wire
   rack and leave to cool. Use the syrup
   as glue if necessary to decorate.

SERVES: 4 | PREP TIME: 50 MINS

White Chocolate Mousse

100 g / 3 ½ oz / ½ cup good quality white chocolate, broken into pieces

250 ml / 9 oz / 1 cup double (heavy) cream

2 egg whites

1 tbsp caster (superfine) sugar

2 tbsp white chocolate shavings

1. Break the chocolate into small pieces and place in a bowl with the cream. Place over a pan of simmering water and whisk until the chocolate has melted. Remove from the heat, leave to cool and then chill for at least 30 minutes.

2. Whisk the egg whites, adding the sugar as you whisk, until thick and glossy. Whisk the chocolate mixture until the mixture forms soft peaks, then fold the egg whites in a third at a time, being careful not to lose the air.

3. Spoon into individual ramekins or dessert glasses and chill in the refrigerator until needed.

4. Serve garnished with shavings of white chocolate.

SERVES: 6 | **PREP TIME: 20 MINS** | **COOKING TIME: 40 MINS**

Sticky Toffee Pudding

FOR THE SPONGE
75 g / 2 ½ oz / ⅓ cup dates, stoned and
   finely chopped
1 tsp bicarbonate of soda
50 g / 1 ¾ oz / ¼ cup butter
pinch of salt
150 g / 5 oz / ⅔ cup Demerara sugar
2 eggs
175 g / 6 oz / ¾ cup self-raising flour
1 tsp vanilla extract
butter, softened

FOR THE SAUCE
250 ml / 9 fl. oz / 1 cup double
   (heavy) cream
80 g / 2 ½ oz / ⅓ cup butter
80 g / 2 ½ oz / ⅓ cup dark brown sugar

1. Preheat the oven to 180°C (160°C fan) / 350F / gas 4.

2. Pour 275 ml / 10 fl. oz / 1 cup boiling water into a bowl and add the dates to soak.

3. When the water is lukewarm, add the remaining sponge ingredients, mixing well
   to combine.

4. Pour into a buttered baking dish and bake in the oven for about 40 minutes,
   or until just firm.

5. Heat the sauce ingredients in a pan, whisking regularly.

6. When the sponge is cooked, pour over the sauce and flash briefly under a hot
   grill until bubbling.

7. Serve with ice cream or cream.

Lemon Sorbet

500 g / 1 lb / 2 cups caster
  (superfine) sugar
250 ml / 9 fl. oz / 1 cup lemon juice
1 lemon, grated zest

1. Heat the sugar in a pan with 750 ml / 1 ⅓ pints / 3 cups water and stir until dissolved.

2. If the lemon is waxed, dip into boiling water briefly to remove it. Stir in the lemon juice and zest, then leave to cool.

3. Churn in an ice cream machine to a smooth sorbet. Freeze until required.

4. Transfer to the refrigerator 1 hour before eating.

SERVES: **4** | PREP TIME: **10 MINS** | COOKING TIME: **50-60 MINS**

Vanilla Baked Egg Custard

500 ml / 1 pint / 2 cups milk
1 tsp vanilla extract
40 g caster (superfine) sugar
3 eggs, lightly beaten
grated nutmeg

1. Preheat the oven to 180°C (160°C fan) / 350F / gas 5.

2. Heat the milk and vanilla in a pan until nearly at boiling point then set aside to cool for a minute.

3. Meanwhile whisk the sugar with the eggs.

4. Pour the scented milk over the eggs, whisking continually until thickened and smooth.

5. Strain into a buttered oven-proof 1 pint baking dish. Bake for 50–60 minutes until just set.

6. Serve with freshly grated nutmeg over the top.

SERVES: 4 | PREP TIME: 20 MINS | COOKING TIME: 1 HOUR 30 MINS

Carrot Cake

300 g / 10 oz / 1 ¼ cups plain (all-purpose) flour
1 tsp ground cinnamon
1 tsp baking powder
½ tsp bicarbonate of soda
200 g / 7 oz / ¾ cup soft dark brown sugar
4 eggs
250 ml / 9 fl. oz / 1 cup vegetable oil
zest of 2 oranges
200 g / 7 oz / ¾ cup carrots, peeled and grated
125 g / 4 oz / ½ cup butter, softened
2 tbsp icing (confectioner's) sugar
250 g / 9 oz / 1 cup cream cheese
zest of ½ lemon

1. Preheat the oven to 150°C (130°C fan) / 300F / gas 2. Grease and line a 20 cm (8 in) cake tin.

2. Sieve the flour into a bowl with cinnamon, baking powder and bicarbonate of soda, then stir in the sugar.

3. Beat the eggs with the oil and fold into the flour with the carrots and orange zest.

4. Spoon into the cake tin and bake for around 1 ½ hours until an inserted skewer comes out clean. Leave to cool.

5. Beat the butter and sugar together until pale, then beat in the cream cheese and lemon zest. Chill until spreadable and cover the cake using a palette knife to smooth.

MAKES: **36** | PREP TIME: **45 MINS** | SETTING TIME: **45 MINS**

Vanilla Fudge

300 ml / 10 fl. oz / 1 ¼ cups milk
350 g / 12 oz / 1 ½ cups caster
  (superfine) sugar
100 g / 3 ½ oz / ½ cup butter
1 tsp vanilla extract

1. Lightly grease a 17 cm (7 in) cake tin
   or roasting tin

2. Place the ingredients, except the
   vanilla in a saucepan and heat slowly,
   stirring constantly, until the sugar has
   dissolved and the butter has melted.

3. Bring to the boil and boil for around
   15–20 minutes, stirring constantly,
   until the mixture reaches 'soft ball'
   stage (115°C) or until a small amount
   of mixture dropped into a glass of
   cold water will form a soft ball that
   you can pick up on the end of a
   teaspoon. Remove from the heat,
   stir in the vanilla and leave to cool for
   5 minutes.

4. Using a wooden spoon, beat the
   mixture until it thickens and the
   shine disappears and it starts to look
   more opaque.

5. Pour into the tin and set at room
   temperature for at least 45 minutes.
   Once set, cut into squares and serve.

SERVES: 6 | PREP TIME: 30 MINS | COOKING TIME: 12 MINS

Jam Swiss Roll

100 g / 3 ½ oz / ⅔ cup self-raising flour
1 tsp baking powder
100 g / 3 ½ oz / ½ cup caster (superfine) sugar
100 g / 3 ½ oz/ ½ cup butter
2 large eggs
225 g / 8 oz / ⅔ cup strawberry jam (jelly)
icing (confectioner's) sugar for dusting

TO SERVE
2 tbsp strawberry jam (jelly), sieved
150 g / 5 ½ oz / 1 cup strawberries, quartered
1 mango, peeled, stoned and cut into bite-sized chunks

1. Preheat the oven to 180°C (160°C fan) / 350F / gas 4 and grease and line a
   Swiss roll tin with greaseproof paper.
2. Put the flour, baking powder, sugar, butter and eggs in a large mixing bowl and
   whisk together with an electric whisk for 4 minutes or until pale and well whipped.
3. Spoon the mixture into the tin and spread into an even layer with a palette knife.
   Bake for 12 minutes or until the cake is springy to the touch.
4. Dust a sheet of greaseproof paper with icing sugar. When the cake is ready,
   turn it out onto the paper and peel off the lining paper. Spread the cake with the
   jam, then roll it up tightly and leave to cool.
5. Cut the cake into twelve slices and serve two slices on each plate.
6. Put the jam in a small paper piping bag and pipe a little on each plate, then garnish
   with strawberries and mango and dust lightly with icing sugar.

SERVES: **4** | PREP TIME: **30 MINS** | COOKING TIME: **8 MINS**

Chocolate Fondant Puddings

90 g / 3 oz / ⅓ cup caster (superfine) sugar
150 g / 5 oz / ⅔ cup butter
150 g / 5 oz / ⅔ cup dark chocolate, chopped
3 egg yolks
3 eggs
1 tbsp plain (all-purpose) flour
1 tsp vanilla extract

1. Preheat the oven to 180°C (160°C fan) / 350F / gas 4. Grease four individual dariole moulds.
2. Place the sugar, butter and chocolate in a bowl set over a pan of simmering water and stir occasionally until melted. Remove from the heat and whisk to combine. Leave to cool for 5 minutes.
3. Add the egg yolks and eggs and beat well to combine, then fold in the flour.
4. Pour into the moulds and chill for 20 minutes.
5. Place on a baking tray and cook for 8 minutes.
6. Turn out onto plates and serve immediately.

SERVES: 6 | PREP TIME: 1 HOUR | COOKING TIME: 1 HOUR 10 MINS

Lemon Meringue Pie

125 g / 4 oz / ½ cup plain
(all-purpose) flour
60 g / 2 oz / ¼ cup butter
pinch of salt
cold water

FOR THE FILLING
3 level tbsp cornflour
60 g / 2 oz / ¼ cup caster
(superfine) sugar
300 ml / 10 fl. oz / 1 ¼ cups
cold water
grated zest and juice of
2–3 lemons
2 egg yolks
40 g butter

FOR THE MERINGUE
2 egg whites
120 g / 4 oz / ½ cup caster
(superfine) sugar

1. Preheat the oven to 190°C (170°C fan) / 370F / gas 5.

2. Make the pastry: sieve the flour and salt into a large bowl, then work the fat into the flour with the pads of your fingers until the mixture resembles breadcrumbs.

3. Work in 2 tablespoons of water and bring the mixture together with a knife, cutting it through to mix, using enough water to just make a smooth ball of dough. Wrap the dough in cling film and refrigerate.

4. Roll the pastry out to just larger than your pie dish. Cut an 8 mm strip all round, dampen the rim of the dish and press the pastry strip on to it. Line the tin with the pastry and press the edges onto the pastry rim. Prick the base with a fork and bake for 25 minutes.

5. Place the cornflour and sugar in a bowl and add enough of the water to make a smooth paste. Pour the remaining water into a pan with the lemon zest. Bring to the boil, pour onto the cornflour paste and mix.

6. Tip back into the pan and bring back to the boil for 1 minute. Remove from the heat and beat in the egg yolks, lemon juice and butter. Pour into the pastry shell and spread evenly.

7. Whisk the egg whites until stiff, then beat in sugar at a time until thick and glossy. Spread over the filling, sealing the top completely.

8. Reduce the oven heat to 150°C (130°C fan) / 300F / gas 2 and bake for 45 minutes until the meringue is pale gold.

SERVES: **6-8** | PREP TIME: **40 MINS** | COOKING TIME: **25 MINS**

Victoria Sponge

120 g / 4 oz / ½ cup butter,
  at room temperature
120 g / 4 oz / ½ cup caster
  (superfine) sugar
2 eggs
1 tsp vanilla extract
120 g / 4 oz / ½ cup self-raising flour
raspberry or strawberry jam (jelly)
icing (confectioner's) sugar

1. Preheat the oven to 170°C (150°C fan)
   / 325F / gas 3. Grease and line
   two 17 cm (7 in) sponge tins.

2. Cream the butter and sugar together
   until pale and creamy.

3. Whisk the eggs thoroughly, then beat
   into the butter mixture a little at a
   time until fully incorporated.

4. Stir in the vanilla extract, then sieve
   the flour a little at a time into the bowl
   and fold in with a metal spoon. If the
   batter is a little thick, add a little hot
   water to loosen.

5. Spoon gently into the tins, then bake
   for 25 minutes or until golden.

6. Leave to cool for 10 minutes. Remove
   from the tins and cool on a wire rack.
   Sandwich with the jam and dust with
   icing sugar to serve.

Raspberry Fool

300 g / 10 oz / 1 ¼ cups raspberries
150 ml / 5 fl. oz / ⅔ cup double
  (heavy) cream
125 ml / 4 fl. oz / ½ cup Greek
  natural yogurt
1 tbsp icing (confectioner's) sugar

1. Tip the raspberries into a bowl and lightly crush with a fork so that it is a mixture of liquid and fruit. This will give the fool a more interesting texture.
2. Lightly whip the cream to soft peaks, then fold in the yogurt.
3. Fold the raspberries through to make a ripple effect.
4. Serve in small bowls.

Rice pudding

3 tbsp butter, melted
60 g / 2 oz / ¼ cup pudding rice
30 g caster (superfine) sugar
1 tsp vanilla extract
500 ml / 1 pint / 2 cups full fat milk
fresh nutmeg

1. Preheat the oven to 150°C (130°C fan) / 300F / gas 2.
2. Use half the butter to grease a baking dish.
3. Add the rice, sugar and vanilla extract, then pour over the milk.
4. Top with the remaining melted butter and grate over a little nutmeg.
5. Bake very gently for about 2 hours, stirring every 30 minutes until the milk is absorbed and the rice creamy.

SERVES: **4** | PREP TIME: **20 MINS** | COOKING TIME: **1 HOUR**

Eton Mess

175 g / 6 oz / ¾ cup caster (superfine) sugar
3 egg whites
500 g / 1 lb / 2 cups raspberries,
1 tbsp icing (confectioner's) sugar
500 ml / 1 pint / 2 cups double (heavy) cream
1 tsp vanilla extract

1. Preheat the oven to 150°C (130°C fan) / 300F / gas 2.
2. Whisk the egg whites to soft peaks, then whisk in the sugar a little at a time, beating each addition in thoroughly, until thick and glossy.
3. Spoon onto lined baking trays and bake for 1 hour. Turn the oven off and leave until completely cold.
4. Purée half the raspberries with the icing sugar until smooth.
5. Whisk the cream to soft peaks, whisking in the vanilla as you go.
6. Break up the meringues and layer into individual serving dishes, spooning over a little purée, then adding raspberries and cream.
7. Top with a raspberry and serve immediately.

Banoffee Pie

400 g / 14 oz / 1 ½ cups digestive
  biscuits, crushed
200 g / 7 oz / ⅔ cup butter, melted
2 tins of condensed milk
500 ml / 1 pint / 2 cups double
  (heavy) cream
2–3 ripe bananas
1 tbsp dark chocolate, grated

1. Combine the biscuits and butter in
   a bowl then press into the bottom
   of a springform tin. Refrigerate.

2. Cover the condensed milk tins
   completely in boiling water and boil
   for 2 hours. Make sure they are
   covered at all times, topping up if
   necessary otherwise they will explode.

3. Remove from the water and leave to
   cool. Open the tins and scoop out
   the toffee.

4. Whizz the bananas with a spoonful of
   toffee in a food processor until
   smooth. Whisk the cream to soft peak
   then fold the banana mixture in until
   combined.

5. Spread half the banana cream over
   the biscuit base, then smooth over a
   layer of toffee, using a palette knife
   to even it out. Repeat, leaving a small
   amount of banana cream for piping.

6. Pipe rosettes of banana cream onto
   the top of the toffee, then decorate
   with grated chocolate. Refrigerate.

SERVES: 4-6 | PREP TIME: 15 MINS | COOKING TIME: 30-40 MINS

Bread and Butter Pudding

8 thick slices white bread, thickly buttered

50 g / 1 ¾ oz / ¼ cup sultanas, soaked in a little brandy

300 ml / 10 fl. oz / 1 ¼ cups milk

60 ml / 3 fl. oz / ¼ cup double (heavy) cream

50 g / 1 ¾ oz / ¼ cup caster (superfine) sugar

3 eggs

freshly grated nutmeg

1 baking dish liberally buttered

1. Preheat the oven to 180°C (160°C fan) / 350F / gas 5.

2. Cut each slice of bread into two triangles and arrange a layer in the base of the baking dish.

3. Sprinkle with the soaked sultanas.

4. Add another layer of bread triangles over the top.

5. Whisk together the milk, cream, sugar and eggs until well combined, then pour over the bread layers. Push the bread down into the custard to soak it thoroughly. The custard should just reach the top of the bread – if it doesn't add a little more milk and/or cream.

6. Grate over the nutmeg.

7. Bake in the oven for 30–40 minutes until set and golden.

SERVES: 8-10 | PREP TIME: 30 MINS | COOKING TIME: 30 MINS

Chocolate Fudge Cake

120 g / 4 oz / ½ cup self-raising flour
1 tsp baking powder
120 g / 4 oz / ½ cup butter, softened
120 g / 4 oz / ½ cup caster
  (superfine) sugar
2 eggs
1 ½ tbsp cocoa powder

FOR THE FILLING AND ICING
75 g / 2 ½ oz / ⅓ cup granulated sugar
75 ml / 2 ½ oz / ⅓ cup evaporated milk
120 g / 4 oz / ½ cup dark
  chocolate, chopped
40 g butter, softened
25 g chocolate, shaved

1. Preheat the oven to 170°C (150°C fan) / 325F / gas 3.
2. Grease and line two 17 cm (7 in) cake tins.
3. Sieve the flour and baking powder into a large bowl, then add the other ingredients.
4. Divide the mixture equally between the two cake tins and cook for 30 minutes.
5. Remove from the tins and cool on a wire rack.
6. Make the icing: combine the sugar and evaporated milk in a pan and stir to dissolve the sugar.
7. Bring to the boil and simmer for 5 minutes, then stir in the chocolate and butter. Chill for at least 1 hour until it has thickened and is spreadable.
8. Use the icing to sandwich the cakes together, then smooth the remainder over the top and sides with a palette knife. Decorate with chocolate shavings.

SERVES: **4** | PREP TIME: **25 MINS**

Tiramisu

600 ml / 1 pint / 2 cups double (heavy) cream
250 g / 9 oz / 1 cup mascarpone
3 tbsp Marsala dolce
5 tbsp caster (superfine) sugar
300 ml / 10 fl. oz / 1 ¼ cups strong coffee
2 tbsp coffee liqueur (optional)
175 g / 6 oz sponge fingers (ladyfingers)
25 g dark chocolate, grated
3 tsp cocoa powder

1. Place the cream, mascarpone, Marsala and sugar in a bowl and whisk until combined and thick.

2. Pour the coffee (and liqueur) into a shallow dish and soak the sponge fingers in it, but be careful they don't disintegrate. Layer half the biscuits into a serving dish, then spoon over half the mascarpone mixture. Grate over half of the chocolate. Repeat until all the ingredients are used up.

3. Chill in the refrigerator for 3 hours.

4. Dust with cocoa powder and more chocolate to serve.

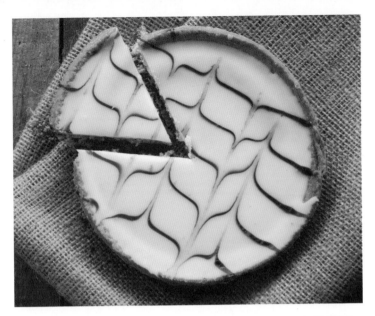

SERVES: 8 | PREP/CHILLING TIME: 1 HOUR 30 MINS | COOKING TIME: 45 MINS

Cherry Bakewell Tart

110 g / 4 oz / ½ cup butter,
  cubed and chilled
225 g / 8 oz / 1 ½ cups plain
  (all purpose) flour
110 g / 4 oz / ½ cup raspberry jam (jelly)
200 g / 7 oz / 2 cups icing
  (confectioner's) sugar
1 tbsp unsweetened cocoa powder

FOR THE FRANGIPANE
55 g / 2 oz / ½ cup ground almonds
55 g / 2 oz / ¼ cup caster
  (superfine) sugar
55 g / 2 oz / ¼ cup butter, softened
1 large egg
1 tsp almond essence

1. Rub the butter into the flour. Add just enough cold water to bind the mixture together into a dough.

2. Roll out the pastry on a floured surface and use it to line a 23 cm (9 in) round tart case. Leave the pastry to chill in the fridge for 30 minutes.

3. Preheat the oven to 200°C (180°C fan) / 400F / gas 6. Line the pastry case with clingfilm, fill it with baking beans, then bake for 15 minutes.

4. To make the frangipane, combine all the ingredients in a bowl and whisk together until smooth.

5. When the pastry case is ready, remove the clingfilm and baking beans. Spread the base with jam. Top with the frangipane mixture and bake for 30 minutes. Leave to cool.

6. Sieve 150 g of icing sugar into a bowl and stir in warm water, 1 teaspoon at a time, to make a thick icing. Put the rest in a different bowl with the cocoa and repeat to make the chocolate icing.

7. Spread the plain icing over the tart in an even layer. Put the chocolate icing in a small piping bag and pipe parallel lines across the top. Drag a toothpick across the chocolate lines to feather, changing direction each time.

8. Leave to set before serving.

Index